OUT OF THE LAB
EXTREME JOBS IN SCIENCE

ASTRONOMERS

by Ruth Owen

PowerKiDS
press

New York

Published in 2014 by The Rosen Publishing Group, Inc.
29 East 21st Street, New York, NY 10010

First Edition

Produced for Rosen by Ruby Tuesday Books Ltd
Editor for Ruby Tuesday Books Ltd: Mark J. Sachner
US Editor: Joshua Shadowens
Designer: Tammy West and Emma Randall

Photo Credits:
Cover, 4, © Superstock; cover, 5, © Shutterstock; 1, 14–15, 28–29 © United States Antarctic Program; 6–7, 8–9, © Wikipedia Creative Commons; 9 (top)© European Southern Observatory; 11, 12–13, 22–23, 24–25, 26–27 © NASA; 16–17, 19, 21 © IceCube South Pole Neutrino Observatory.

Publisher Cataloging Data

Owen, Ruth.
Astronomers / by Ruth Owen. — First edition.
    p. cm. — (Out of the lab: extreme jobs in science)
Includes index.
ISBN 978-1-4777-1289-4 (library binding) — ISBN 978-1-4777-1378-5 (pbk.) — ISBN 978-1-4777-1379-2 (6-pack)
1. Astronomers — Juvenile literature. 2. Astronomy — Juvenile literature. 3. Astronomy — Vocational guidance — Juvenile literature. I. Owen, Ruth, 1967–. II. Title.
QB35.O94 2014
520.23—dc23

Manufactured in the United States of America

CPSIA Compliance Information: Batch #S13PK8: For Further Information contact Rosen Publishing, New York, New York at 1-800-237-9932

Contents

WHAT IS AN ASTRONOMER?

Astronomy is the scientific study of objects in outer space, such as planets, **asteroids**, stars, **galaxies**, and everything that exists outside of Earth's **atmosphere**.

Astronomers are scientists who study outer space. Most astronomers observe objects in space with very large telescopes. For hundreds of years, astronomers used only telescopes that detected the **visible light** waves given off by these objects. These telescopes, called optical telescopes, create greatly magnified images of distant planets, stars, and galaxies.

An astronomer working outdoors with optical telescopes.

Today, astronomers also use telescopes that detect other kinds of light waves that are invisible to the human eye. These waves include X-rays, ultraviolet light, and infrared light. These waves can be used to discover objects that are distant and very faint.

A huge radio telescope in New Mexico

SCIENCE IN ACTION

Radio waves carry wireless electrical signals in TV remotes and cell phones, but they also exist in nature. Distant stars and galaxies are huge sources of powerful radio waves. Astronomers use special telescopes, called radio telescopes, to gather these signals and learn more about space.

AN EXTREME WORKPLACE

Astronomy can be extreme, even on an ordinary day, or night, since that's when most astronomers do their viewing!

For one thing, astronomers are gazing at objects billions of miles (km) from Earth. Also, the observatories in which astronomers usually work must be away from the lights of cities and towns. This means that observatories, and the telescopes they contain, have to be in remote, out of the way places.

Most observatories must also be in high places. This helps stop the effects of Earth's atmosphere from distorting the view an astronomer sees through a telescope. Getting to these remote observatories can take a lot of time and effort.

SCIENCE IN ACTION

The Sphinx Observatory is located in a mountain range in Switzerland. Astronomers visiting the observatory travel into the mountains by train. They then ride up to the observatory in an elevator that has been hollowed out of the inside of the mountain.

The Sphinx Observatory

Observatories are buildings or structures that contain telescopes.

ASTRONOMY IN THE DESERT

The Paranal Observatory, which is operated by the European Southern Observatory, is in the Atacama Desert. The Atacama Desert is the driest desert in the world.

The observatory is situated on a mountain called Cerro Paranal. An astronomer who wants to use the equipment at this observatory begins his or her visit with a flight into Santiago, Chile. The flight is followed by several hours of riding through the Atacama Desert, often on dirt tracks.

Finally, after hours in the dry, barren desert, it's possible to glimpse the observatory's telescopes on top of the mountain. Four of the Paranal Observatory's telescopes are known together as the Very Large Telescope (VLT).

SCIENCE IN ACTION

At the Paranal Observatory, most of the astronomers' work is done at night, for several hours or nights at a time. Then, after collecting and recording data from the telescopes, visiting astronomers begin the long trek home!

The four telescopes that are known
as the Very Large Telescope (VLT)

The Paranal Observatory
in the Atacama Desert

ASTRONOMY IN THE SKIES

Most astronomers look at the night sky through telescopes on the ground. A lucky few, however, get to observe space from high above the Earth's surface.

An airborne observatory is a plane that has been specially adapted to carry a telescope and other equipment for investigating space. The plane flies at **altitudes** of up to 48,000 feet (14,630 m), or 9 miles (14.5 km). From this height above Earth, the plane's telescope can observe outer space without the **distortion** caused by **water vapor** in Earth's atmosphere.

On a seven-hour night-time flight, a small group of astronomers gets the chance to use the plane's telescope and carry out experiments and investigations. Flying miles (km) above the Earth, a flying observatory is an exciting and extreme place to work!

SCIENCE IN ACTION

Airborne observatories sometimes fly so high that the plane's crew and the scientists working on board have to wear oxygen masks.

The SOFIA airborne observatory

SOFIA's telescope

This photo of Halley's Comet crossing the Milky Way was taken by the Kuiper Airborne Observatory (KAO).

AIRBORNE OBSERVATORIES

Lockheed C-141 Starlifters were cargo planes flown by the US Air Force. Their missions were to airlift soldiers and weapons over great distances.

In the 1970s, **NASA** converted one of these military planes into a flying observatory. The plane's name was the Kuiper Airborne Observatory, or KAO. From 1974 to 1995, astronomers aboard KAO flew about 70 missions per year. The scientists made many important and exciting discoveries.

The KAO has now been replaced by a technologically advanced plane called SOFIA (the **Stratospheric** Observatory for Infrared Astronomy). SOFIA completed its first test flight in 2007, and its telescope is scheduled to be in full operation in 2014. The plane will then fly astronomers on about 100 research missions each year.

SCIENCE IN ACTION

Astronomers aboard KAO made many discoveries about our home galaxy, the Milky Way. They also discovered that the dwarf planet Pluto has an atmosphere and that the planet Uranus has rings.

The Kuiper Airborne Observatory

Scientists test equipment aboard the SOFIA airborne observatory

ASTRONOMY AT THE SOUTH POLE

Some astronomers and scientists get to work in Antarctica at the South Pole. These astronomers work at the IceCube South Pole **Neutrino** Observatory.

IceCube is an unusual telescope, or detector, that looks for neutrinos. Neutrinos are tiny particles that are constantly traveling through space. They travel in straight lines at the **speed of light**, and nothing stops them from moving. In fact, about 100 trillion neutrinos are passing through your body every second!

The scientists that work at IceCube study neutrinos because they can reveal information about the **universe**, including how it came into being. There is so much that scientists still don't know about the universe that studying neutrinos may help solve many mysteries.

Antarctica is the coldest and perhaps most extreme place on Earth. The average temperature in winter is around −100°F (−73°C).

Scott Smith, a scientist at IceCube, gets frosty on a South Pole spring day.

This is the laboratory at the IceCube South Pole Neutrino Observatory.

ICECUBE

The IceCube telescope uses ice to capture information from neutrinos, which is why it was built in Antarctica. Here, the ice can be miles (km) deep.

IceCube is made up of 86 cables that are buried deep in ice. On each cable there are 60 basketball-sized sensors, called Digital Optical Modules (DOMs). These sensors detect light from neutrinos. The cables and DOMs are buried up to 1.5 miles (2.45 km) beneath the ice.

When a neutrino travels through ice and interacts with an ice **atom**, a blue light is produced. When this happens in the ice surrounding IceCube, the DOM sensors detect the light. IceCube's scientists then use the light to find out where in the universe the neutrino came from and other pieces of important data.

A drill making a hole in the ice for one of IceCube's cables.

The deep holes for IceCube's cables were drilled in the ice with special drills. The drills use hot water to melt the ice and create a hole.

This diagram shows how IceCube looks under the ice.

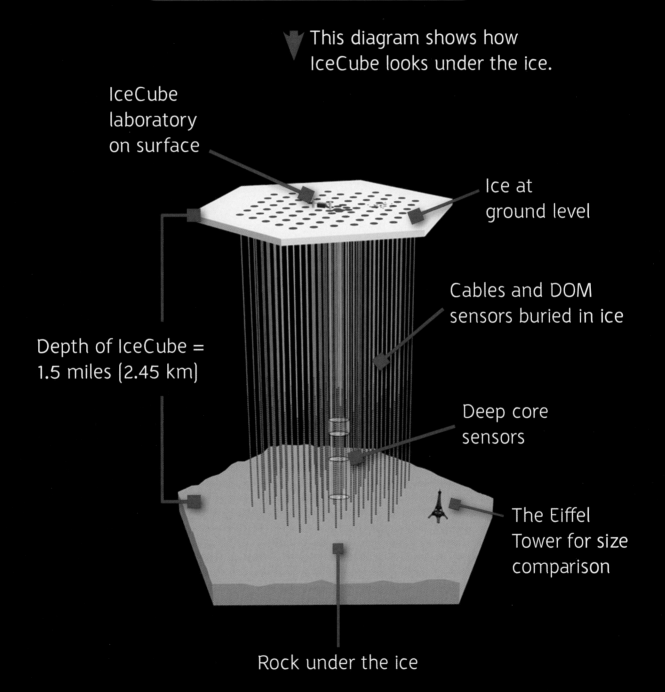

IceCube laboratory on surface

Ice at ground level

Cables and DOM sensors buried in ice

Depth of IceCube = 1.5 miles (2.45 km)

Deep core sensors

The Eiffel Tower for size comparison

Rock under the ice

MEET THE CUBERS

The astronomers and other scientists who work at IceCube are known as "Cubers."

To be a Cuber, a person must be fit and healthy. There are doctors at the South Pole, but if a serious illness occurs, the patient is many hours from a hospital. So all Cubers undergo a health check before they travel to the South Pole.

A mission to IceCube begins with a flight to New Zealand. Here, the Cubers are provided with cold-weather clothing. Then, it's another flight to the McMurdu station on the coast of Antarctica. From McMurdu, the scientists fly inland to the South Pole Station, where IceCube is located. After, a journey that can last 72 hours, Cubers finally arrive at the South Pole.

SCIENCE IN ACTION

People, fuel, food, and all other supplies have to be flown in to the South Pole Station. To keep the Antarctic clean and pollution free, all the station's garbage is flown out.

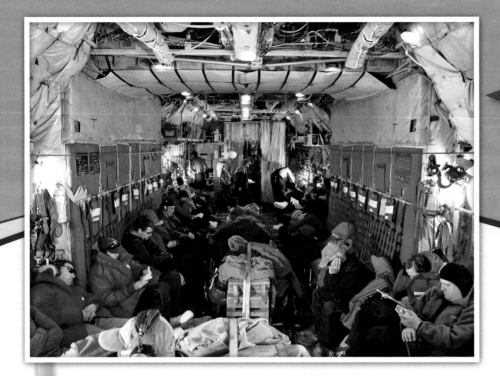

Cubers aboard the plane to the South Pole Station. Travel to IceCube isn't glamorous!

The plane that carries people from McMurdu to the South Pole Station is fitted with skis for landing on ice.

LIFE AT ICECUBE

The South Pole Station has living space for around 200 people. Some are Cubers, and others are scientists visiting the South Pole to do other types of research.

The station has a large kitchen with cooks to provide all the food, a dining room, places where people can relax, and even a gym. There is also a greenhouse for growing vegetables to add to the food supplies.

When Cubers aren't carrying out research in the IceCube laboratory, they can visit the gym, play games, watch movies, or shoot pool. Sometimes the astronomers and scientists give talks to each other about their projects.

SCIENCE IN ACTION

It's so cold at the South Pole that thawing frozen food can take up to a week! If you feel like having some ice cream, you have to remove it from the freezer several hours before you want to eat.

Time for fun: Some Cubers take part in a South Pole New Year's parade.

Time for work: A scientist analyzes data collected by IceCube.

METEORITE HUNTERS

Some of the space scientists who work in the extreme conditions of Antarctica are **meteorite** hunters.

Meteorites are small chunks of rock that land on Earth from outer space. Antarctica is the best place in the world to find meteorites. On other continents, meteorites get worn away by weather. They may also be buried under roads or buildings because people think they are ordinary rocks. In Antarctica, a meteorite can fall to Earth and then stay safely buried under ice and snow for thousands of years.

When meteorite hunters find a **specimen**, they handle it with stainless steel instruments. It is put it into a plastic or foil package to keep it from becoming contaminated. Then it is sent to a laboratory to be studied and analyzed.

Meteorites are sometimes formed when large asteroids collide and break apart, as shown in this artwork.

Meteorite hunters have found rocks from the Moon and Mars in Antarctica. Studying meteorites gives scientists a chance to analyze a piece of rock that has come from another world.

▲ Scientists carefully collect a meteorite specimen.

SEEING SPACE FROM SPACE

Astronomer Tamara Jernigan didn't just observe space from Earth. Tamara, known as Tammy, went into space as a space shuttle astronaut and even performed a space walk!

Tammy was in the Astronauts Corps between 1969 and 2001. She flew on five Space Shuttle missions. During her Space Shuttle flights, Tammy carried out investigations into how space flight affects humans, animals, and **cells**. She studied **radiation** coming from distant stars and galaxies, and researched what stars are made of and how they form.

In 1995, Tammy spent nearly 17 days aboard the Space Shuttle *Endeavour*. Along with two fellow crew members, she operated three telescopes that were aboard the spacecraft.

Astronomer and astronaut Tammy Jernigan

The Space Shuttle *Discovery* blasts off on May 27, 1999. There are seven astronauts aboard, including Tammy Jernigan.

SCIENCE IN ACTION

Tammy Jernigan spent 63 days, 1 hour, and 24 minutes in space during her career as an astronaut.

WALKING IN SPACE

In May and June 1999, Tammy Jernigan flew a 10-day mission on the Space Shuttle *Discovery*.

On this mission, *Discovery*'s crew performed the first-ever docking to the International Space Station (ISS). *Discovery* connected to the ISS, and then its team of astronauts delivered equipment and supplies onto the space station. The supplies would be needed by future astronaut crews living on the ISS.

During the mission, Tammy and fellow astronaut Daniel Barry also carried out a spacewalk. Attached to the spacecraft with safety lines, Tammy and Daniel worked outside the shuttle. Among their tasks, the two astronauts had to attach two small cranes to the ISS, and hang bags of tools on the space station that future spacewalkers might need.

SCIENCE IN ACTION

As Tammy Jernigan left the Space Shuttle to carry out her spacewalk, she had just one word to say, "Unbelievable!" The space walk lasted for seven hours and 55 minutes.

Tammy Jernigan
during her spacewalk
outside the Space
Shuttle *Discovery*
on May 30, 1999.

EXTREME SCIENCE IN ACTION

Looking at space through a telescope may not seem very extreme. It depends, however, on where that telescope is situated!

Some astronomers get to observe space from remote mountains, from high above Earth in planes, and even from space.

The IceCube laboratory at night. During the winter, it is dark day and night at the South Pole.

They travel to the world's hottest, coldest, and most uncomfortable places. For example, at IceCube in the South Pole, the observatory is situated so high above **sea level** that the air is thin. This makes it difficult to breathe and can make some people feel sick.

For an astronomer, the discomfort of working in an extreme environment is worth it, however, if that place offers the best view of our universe. With so much still to be discovered, every astronomer wants to be the one to solve the next big space mystery!

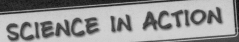

SCIENCE IN ACTION

Working as a scientist in a remote place such as the South Pole can be tough because you have to be away from your home and family for months at a time!

GLOSSARY

altitudes (AL-tuh-toodz) The heights of objects above sea level, or above the ground.

asteroids (AS-the-royds) Rocky objects orbiting the Sun and ranging in size from a few feet (m) to hundreds of miles (km) in diameter.

astronomers (uh-STRAH-nuh-merz) Scientists who specialize in the study of outer space.

atmosphere (AT-muh-sfeer) The layer of gases surrounding a planet, moon, or star.

atom (A-tem) The smallest particle of something, consisting of electrons, protons, and neutrons.

cells (SELZ) The smallest units, or parts, that make up living things.

distortion (dih-STAWRT-shun) A change in the shape of something.

galaxies (GA-lik-sees) Groups of stars, dust, gas, and other objects held together in outer space by gravity.

meteorite (MEE-tee-uh-ryt) A piece of rock, for example from an asteroid, that has survived the fall to the surface of a planet or moon.

NASA (NAS-ah) The National Aeronautics and Space Administration, an organization in the United States that studies space and builds spacecraft.

neutrino (noo-TREE-noh) A tiny, fast-moving particle in space that can come from many different sources, including the Sun, black holes, and supernovas. A supernova occurs when a star explodes and dies.

observatories (ub-ZUR-vuh-tor-eez) Buildings or structures that house telescopes.

radiation (ray-dee-AY-shun) Energy that is radiated in particles, or waves, for example, light from the Sun is radiated in waves.

sea level (SEE LEH-vul) The surface of the sea. It is used as a starting point for measuring the height of land and mountains.

specimen (SPES-men) A sample of something or an item to be scientifically studied.

speed of light (SPEED UV LYT) The speed at which light travels, which is 186,500 miles per second (300,000 km/s). Light is the fastest thing we know of.

stratospheric (stra-tus-FEER-ik) Having to do with the stratosphere, which is the second major layer of Earth's atmosphere (going upward, away from Earth).

universe (YOO-nih-vers) All of the matter and energy that exists as a whole, including gravity and all the planets, stars, galaxies, and contents of intergalactic space.

visible light (VIH-zih-bul LYT) Also simply known as "light," a form of electromagnetic radiation, or energy, that is visible to the human eye, and is responsible for the sense of sight.

water vapor (WAH-tur VAY-pur) The state of water, caused by evaporation, in which it ceases being a liquid and becomes a gas.

WEBSITES

Due to the changing nature of Internet links, PowerKids Press has developed an online list of websites related to the subject of this book. This site is updated regularly. Please use this link to access the list:

www.powerkidslinks.com/olejs/astro/

READ MORE

Nelson, Maria. *Life on the International Space Station.* Extreme Jobs in Extreme Places. New York: Gareth Stevens Learning Library, 2013.

Solway, Andrew. *Quantum Leaps and Big Bangs!* : A History of Astronomy. Stargazers' Guide. Mankato, MN: Heinemann-Raintree, 2006.

Spilsbury, Louise. *How to Survive in the Arctic and Antarctic.* Tough Guides. New York: PowerKids Press, 2012.

INDEX